D1642343

ELIN	
Z778517	
PETERS	17-Jul-2012
612.88	£10.99

The Five Senses

Touching

Rebecca Rissman

www.raintreepublishers.co.uk
Visit our website to find out more information about Raintree books.

To order:

☎ Phone 0845 6044371
▤ Fax +44 (0) 1865 312263
▧ Email myorders@raintreepublishers.co.uk

Customers from outside the UK please telephone +44 1865 312262

Raintree is an imprint of Capstone Global Library Limited, a company incorporated in England and Wales having its registered office at 7 Pilgrim Street, London EC4V 6LB – Registered company number: 6695582

Edited by Rebecca Rissman and Catherine Veitch
Designed by Ryan Frieson and Kimberly R. Miracle
Original illustrations © Capstone Global Library
Illustrated by Tony Wilson (pp. 11, 12, 22, 23)
Picture research by Tracy Cummins
Originated by Capstone Global Library
Printed in China by South China Printing Company Ltd

ISBN 978 0 431 19481 3 (hardback)
14 13 12 11
10 9 8 7 6 5 4 3 2

ISBN 978 0 431 19487 5 (paperback)
15 14 13 12 11
10 9 8 7 6 5 4 3 2 1

British Library Cataloguing in Publication Data
Rissman, Rebecca
Touching. - (The Five Senses)
612.8'8--dc22
A full catalogue record for this book is available from the British Library.

Acknowledgements
The author and publishers are grateful to the following for permission to reproduce copyright material: Alamy pp. 13 (© Jack Sullivan), 16 (© Kader Meguedad); Corbis pp. 4 (© David P. Hall), 15 (© Andrzej Grygiel/PAP), 20 (© Markus Altmann); Getty Images pp. 5 (MoMo Productions), 6 (Bruno Morandi), 7 (Hitoshi Nishimura), 9 (Keiji Iwai), 10 (Marc Oeder), 14 (Livia Corona), 17 (Mark Hall), 18 (Macduff Everton), 19 (Jose Luis Pelaez); Shutterstock pp. 8 (© Melanie DeFazio), 21 (© Karin Lau), 23 (© Melanie DeFazio).

Cover photograph of a hand touching the surface of still mountain water reproduced with permission of Getty Images (Philip and Karen Smith). Back cover photograph of a girl stroking a kitten reproduced with permission of Shutterstock (© Melanie DeFazio).

The publishers would like to thank Nancy Harris, Yael Biederman, and Matt Siegel for their assistance in the preparation of this book.

Every effort has been made to contact copyright holders of any material reproduced in this book. Any omissions will be rectified in subsequent printings if notice is given to the publisher.

Contents

Senses

We all have five senses.

We use our senses every day.

Touching and seeing are senses.

Tasting, smelling, and hearing are also senses.

How do you touch?

You feel the things you touch.

skin

You feel things on your skin.

Nerves under your skin help you to feel.

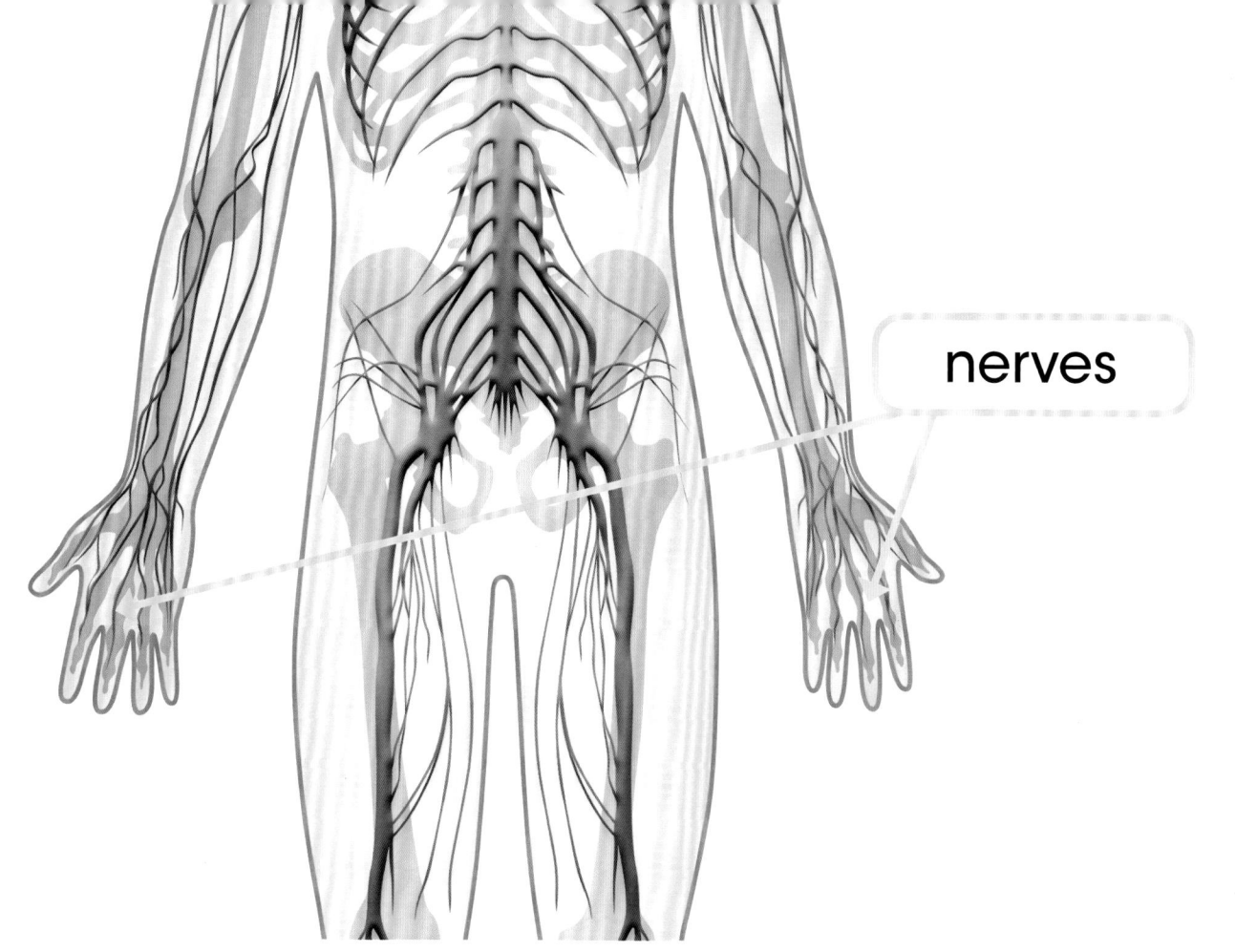

nerves

Nerves are like tiny strings inside our bodies.

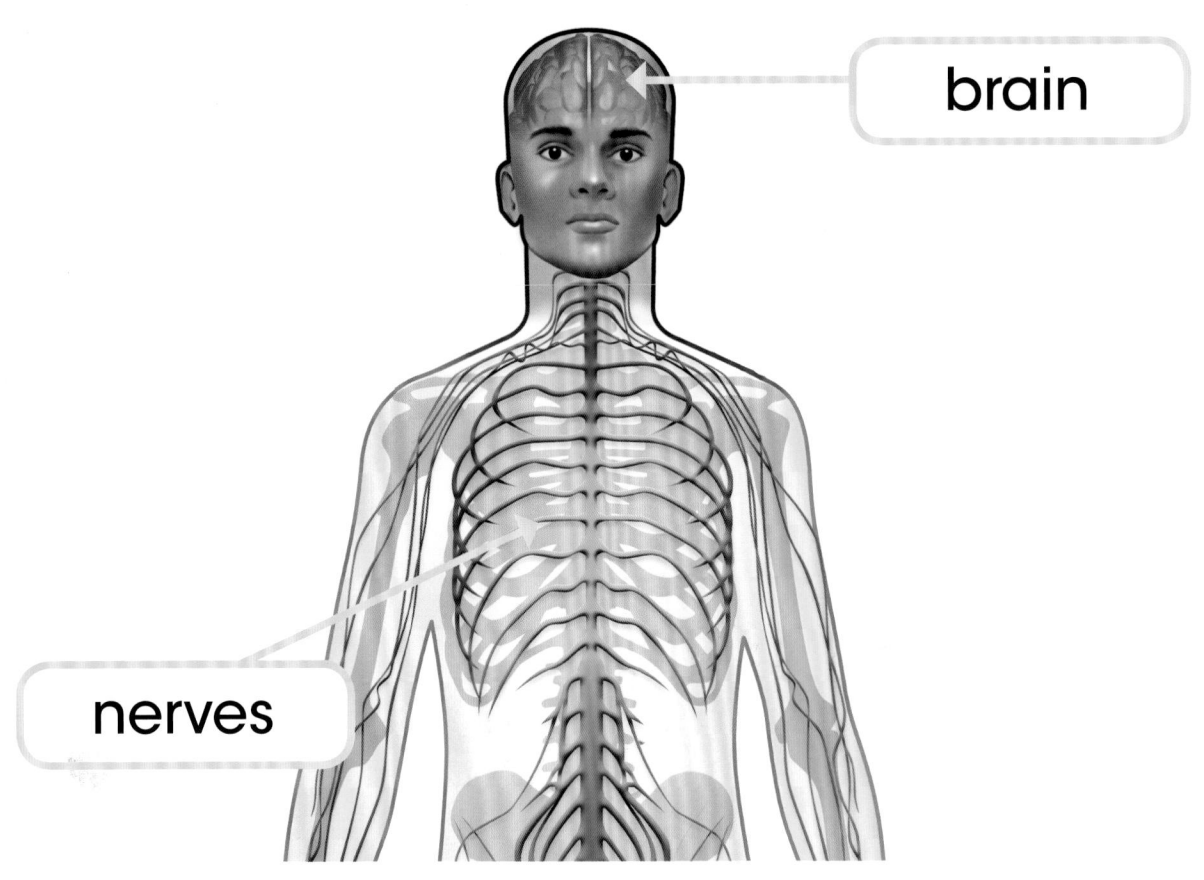

brain

nerves

Nerves tell your brain how things feel.

Your brain tells you what you
are feeling.

What do you touch?

You can touch many different things.

Things can feel very different.

You can touch things that feel
rough. A tree trunk feels rough.

16

You can touch things that feel smooth.
A glass window feels smooth.

You can touch things that feel hot.
Sand can feel hot.

18

You can touch things that feel cold.
Snow feels cold.

Using touch

Some people do not see. They feel the things around them.

They use touch to read.

Naming the parts you use to touch

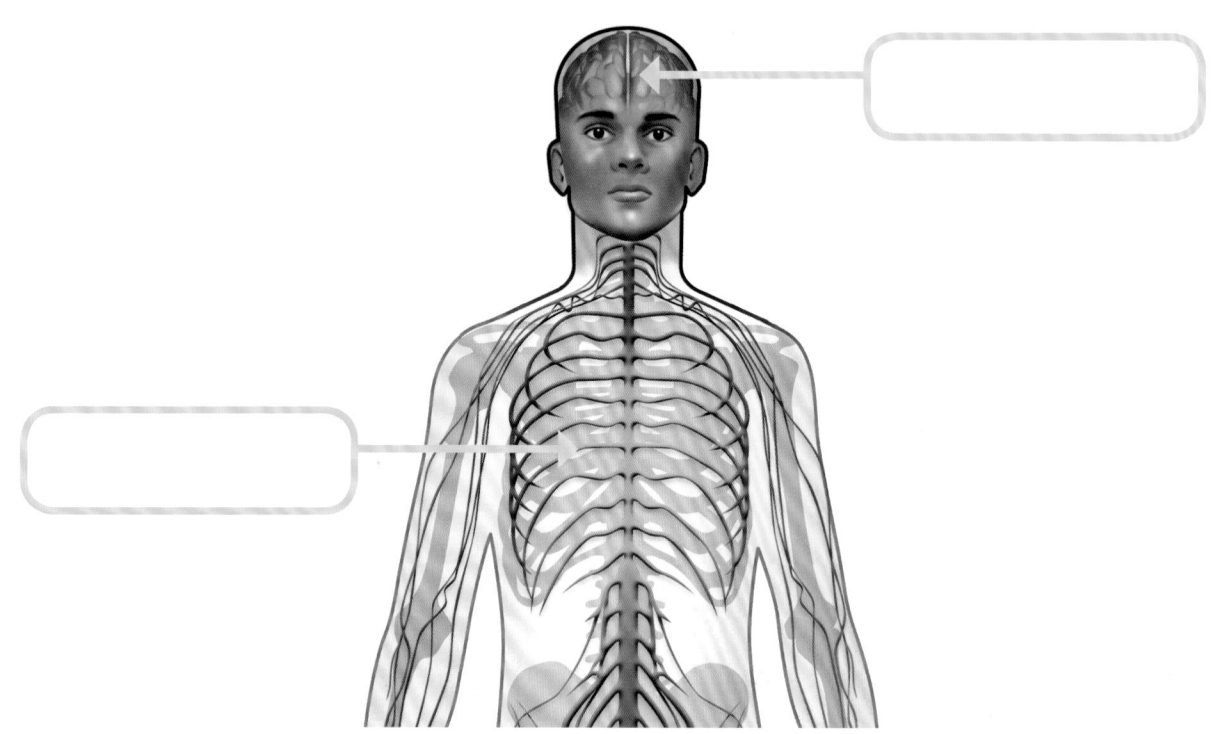

Point to where these labels should go.

brain   nerves

Answer on page 12.

Picture glossary

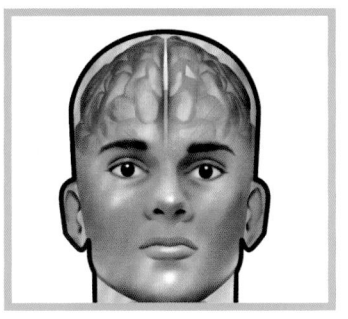

brain part of your body that helps you think, remember, feel, and move

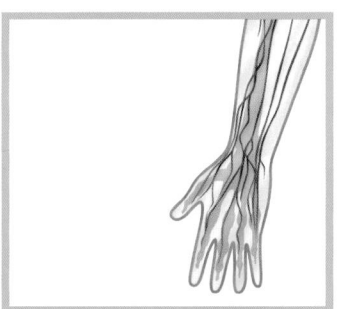

nerves body parts like tiny strings inside you. They carry messages about feelings between your brain and other parts of your body.

sense something that helps you smell, see, touch, taste, or hear things around you

Index

Note to parents and teachers

Before reading

Explain to children that people use five senses to understand the world: seeing, hearing, tasting, touching, and smelling. Tell children that there are different body parts associated with each sense. Then ask children which body parts they think they use to touch. Tell children they use their skin to touch things. Explain that nerves that run under the skin send messages to the brain.

After reading

• Show children the diagram of the sensory system on page 22. Ask them to point to where the labels "brain" and "nerves" should go.

• Make a "feeling box" to put objects in. Ask children to put their hand in the box and feel what's inside. Can they guess what's in the box? Can they describe it?

• Ask children to work in pairs, with one child wearing a blindfold. Ask the other child in each pair to help their partner feel their way around the room. How did the child wearing the blindfold feel? Did feeling things help them to guess where they were?